T0384290

ADA TWIST, SCIENTIST
THE WHY FILES

THE SCIENCE OF **BAKING**

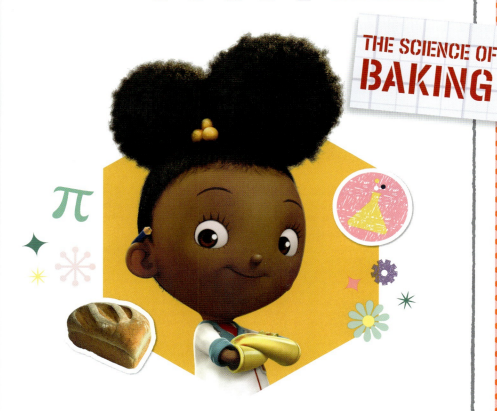

By Andrea Beaty and Dr. Theanne Griffith

Amulet Books • New York

To Katie —A.B.

To Violeta and Lila, my budding bakers —T.G.

PUBLISHER'S NOTE: This is a work of fiction. Names, characters, places, and incidents are either the product of the author's imagination or used fictitiously, and any resemblance to actual persons, living or dead, business establishments, events, or locales is entirely coincidental.

Library of Congress Control Number 2022932922

ISBN 978-1-4197-6153-9

ADA TWIST ™ Netflix. Used with permission.
Story and text © Andrea Beaty
ADA TWIST series imagery © Netflix, Inc. and used with permission from Netflix.
Ada Twist, Scientist and the Questioneers created by Andrea Beaty and David Roberts

Book design by Charice Silverman
Illustrations by Steph Stilwell

Published in 2022 by Amulet Books, an imprint of ABRAMS. All rights reserved. No portion of this book may be reproduced, stored in a retrieval system, or transmitted in any form or by any means, mechanical, electronic, photocopying, recording, or otherwise, without written permission from the publisher.

Printed and bound in U.S.A.

10 9 8 7 6 5 4 3 2 1

Amulet Books are available at special discounts when purchased in quantity for premiums and promotions as well as fundraising or educational use. Special editions can also be created to specification. For details, contact specialsales@abramsbooks.com or the address below.

Amulet Books® is a registered trademark of Harry N. Abrams, Inc.

Images courtesy Shutterstock.com: **Cover:** *bread,* Diana Taliun; *bread baking dish;* TYNZA; *cake,* Anna Shepulova. **Cover, Page 3:** Jfunk. **Page 2:** *bao,* UKIVI; *baguettes,* pixaroma; *naan,* DronG; *nut bread,* CaseyMartin. **Page 5:** *flour,* Africa Studio; *butter,* Tanya Sid; *baking powder/soda,* focal point. **Page 6:** *baguettes,* pixaroma; *cake,* Alexandra Harashchenko. **Page 7:** *flour,* Pinkyone. **Page 8:** *pizza or pizza dough,* Vladislav Noseek. **Page 10:** *dough,* Gap Romaniia. **Page 11:** *various flours and/or almonds, oats, rice,* baibaz; *cake,* Africa Studio. **Page 12:** Jiri Hera. **Page 14:** *baguettes,* LStockStudio. **Page 16:** *sugar in bags or cubes, brown sugar and white sugar,* fotorince. **Page 18:** *butter and oil,* Charlotte Lake; *bread dough being stretched,* Zagorulko Inka. **Page 22:** iva. **Page 23:** *egg white meringue,* Olga Dubravina. **Page 26:** *milk,* DONOT6_STUDIO; *muffins,* Kostina IG. **Page 28:** *baking powder and baking soda,* Naviya. **Page 31:** Andrei Dubadzel. **Page 32:** *dinner rolls,* Maria C Fields. **Page 35:** *jar of sourdough starter,* Gajus. **Page 37:** *jar of sourdough starter,* Zagorulko Inka. **Page 41:** *map pointing to Syria,* Porcupen. **Page 43:** inspiredbyart. **Page 44:** *baguettes,* pixaroma. **Pages 46, 47:** Africa Studio. **Page 51:** Alexeysun. **Pages 52, 53:** Elena Zajchikova. **Page 55:** Zagorulko Inka. **Page 62:** *sugar, water, baking powder, baking soda,* Olga Dubravina; *measuring cups, spoons, and scales,* Cattlaya Art; *measuring cups, spoons, and scales,* Michelle Lee Photography. *Images courtesy Public Domain:* **Cover:** *cake plate top,* Bakewell, Pears and Company. **Cover, Page 5:** *eggs,* Evan-Amos. **Pages i, 13:** AlLes. **Page 8:** *pizza or pizza dough.* **Page 9:** imazite. **Page 14:** *cake,* Annie Spratt. **Page 16:** *sugar in bags or cubes, brown sugar and white* sugar, kalhh. **Page 19:** Batholith. **Page 20:** *eggs,* ViacheslavVladmirivichNetsvetaev; *chicken,* Pava. **Page 23:** *egg yolks,* ponce-photography. **Page 25:** *milk,* Daria-Yakovleva; *milk and dough,* רימזה טע. **Page 28:** *baking powder,* Lou Sander. **Page 29:** *sliced bread,* Daniel Sone. **Page 30:** *baking powder/soda,* Monfocus; *bread,* Scott Bauer, U.S. Department of Agriculture. **Page 32:** *yeast,* tombock1. **Page 51:** *baking powder/soda,* NatureFriend. **Page 60:** U.S. Navy photo by Photographer's Mate Airman Joshua Kinter.

ABRAMS The Art of Books
195 Broadway, New York, NY 10007
abramsbooks.com

I made a cake for my dad's birthday. I put in all the right things, but it tasted terrible! **Why?**

It's a mystery! A riddle! A puzzle! A quest!

Time to find out what baking is about!

Baking is an activity shared by countries all over the world. From bao to baguettes, naan to nut bread, baking plays an important role in all cultures.

Did you know that science plays a big part in baking? There are many ways that bakers use science to make the tastiest of treats!

Each time you bake, you are conducting a small experiment. What happens if you use too much of this or too little of that?

No matter what you decide to bake, you will probably use some of these common ingredients.

THE WHY FILES

FAcTS

COMMON INGREDIENTS IN BAKING

- **FLOUR**

- **FAT**
(like butter or oil)

- **EGGS**

- **LIQUID**
(like milk or water)

- **RAISING AGENT** (like baking powder, baking soda, or yeast)

RAISING AGENT

LIQUID

FAT

FLOUR

EGGS

①

These ingredients are mixed to make a dough. Not all baked goods use every one of these ingredients. You don't use eggs to make pizza dough, and many cakes can be made without butter or oil.

But each of these items has a special and important role in baking. And bakers are always testing new ways of combining them to make yummy goodies!

One ingredient in nearly every baked good is **flour**, and there are many types. Seeds, grains, beans, or nuts are ground up into a fine powder to make flour.

Put me in the blender!

One of the most common types of flour is made from wheat. But bakers often use flour made from almonds, oats, and rice, too!

WHY DO BAKERS USE FLOUR?

Flour helps give dough its shape. There are proteins in flour that come together to become firm when water or milk is added.

Proteins are like building blocks that make things strong. Things like your muscles! And dough.

The more flour used in a recipe, the firmer the dough will be. Bread recipes use more flour than cake recipes. That is one reason breads are firmer than cakes.

soft

firm

I have a theory! Bread has the same ingredients as cake, so if I put icing on bread, it will be a cake!

Sugar is another important baking ingredient. It makes baked goods sweet. Yum! But sugar also changes how baked goods feel.

Cakes are made of similar amounts of flour and sugar. This makes them soft and moist. Bread recipes only use a little bit of sugar compared to flour. This is another reason bread is firmer than cake.

Sugar also makes baked goods turn brown as they cook.

Bakers also use **fats** like butter and oil to help keep breads moist and soft. Fats make the firm proteins in flour more stretchy and flexible. They help make bread bouncy!

stretchy and flexible!

Eggs hold the different ingredients in a recipe together. Just like sugar and fats, they make baked goods moist. Eggs are made of three different parts.

THE WHY FILES
F Ac T S

PARTS OF AN EGG

- The egg **SHELL** is the outer part of an egg. In protects the inside of the egg from damage.

- The egg **WHITE** is clear and is made of mostly water and protein.

- The egg **YOLK** is yellow and found in the middle of an egg. It is made of mostly fat and protein.

20

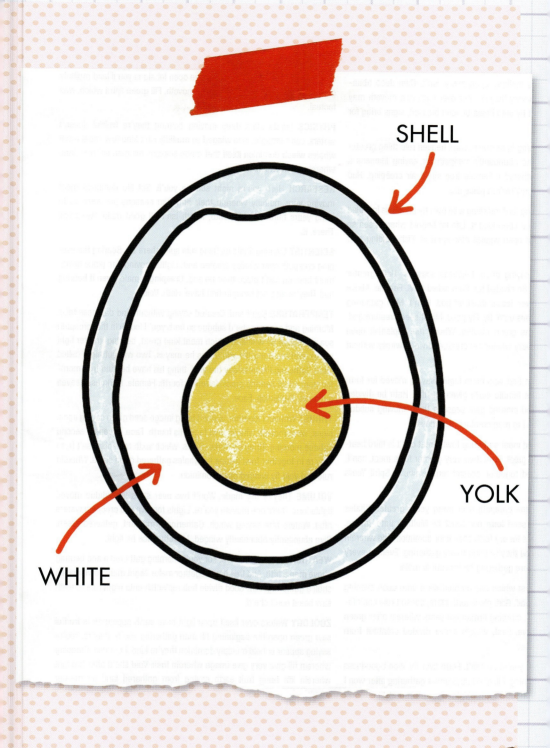

SHELL

YOLK

WHITE

Bakers use both egg whites and egg yolks. Sometimes they use each separately. And sometimes they use them together! It all depends on the result they want.

Egg yolks add fat and flavor to dough. Since egg whites are mostly water, they can be whipped to create a foam that makes dough light and fluffy.

HOW CAN YOU TELL IF AN EGG IS FRESH?

If you put an egg in a bowl of water and it sinks and lays on its side, it is fresh. If it floats, it is rotten.

Water and milk are common **liquids** used in baking. Liquids wet the dry ingredients, like flour, so they can be mixed.

Most bread recipes use water. On the other hand, sweeter baked goods (like muffins!) are often made with milk.

? ?

COMPOSITION of MILK

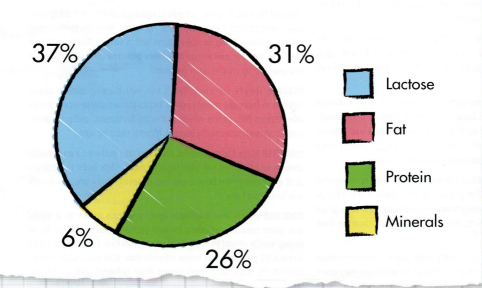

37%

31%

6%

26%

- Lactose
- Fat
- Protein
- Minerals

Milk has sugars, proteins, and fats that are not in water. The sugars in milk add a bit of sweetness to the dough. The proteins make it stronger. The fats help make sure those strong proteins are still flexible. (Muffins taste better when they are soft!)

Cake batter is goopy.
SO HOW DO CAKES BECOME FLUFFY?

Baking powder is another important ingredient used to make baked goods. When baking powder mixes with liquid, little air bubbles are created. As those bubbles get bigger, they make the dough get bigger, too! This is called *rising*.

The space that air bubbles create in the dough makes it nice and fluffy.

A different ingredient called **baking soda** can also be added to a dough to help it rise.

What else do bakers use to help dough rise? Yeast!

ALL ABOUT YEAST

- They are alive! Yeast are living things.

- Yeast are a fungi, like mushrooms!

- Yeast are tiny. If you lined them up, it would take about 8,500 yeast to make an inch!

- They're everywhere! Yeast are in the air, on our skin, and even on trees!

- Yeast need to eat. One of their favorite foods is sugar!

- Bakers use yeast to make breads like dinner rolls rise.

When you mix dry yeast with liquid and sugar, the yeast begin to eat the sugar. This causes them to release gas. Like little yeast burps!

Just as with baking powder and baking soda, those air bubbles make the dough rise.

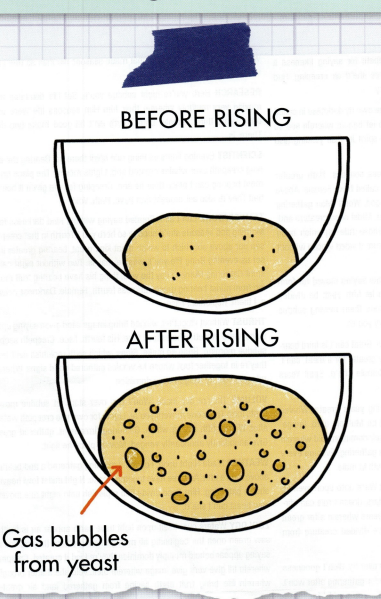

BEFORE RISING

AFTER RISING

Gas bubbles from yeast

A kind of bread called **sourdough** uses yeast in a special way. Instead of mixing dry yeast with sugar water, the recipe uses **wild yeast**.

Wild yeast are found naturally in the environment. In fact, the flour you buy at the grocery store has wild yeast in it!

When you mix a little bit of flour with water, those wild yeast in the flour begin to grow. After a few days of growing, the mix turns into a **sourdough starter**. It's like a yeast soup!

Hunting the Wild Yeast

But there is more than just yeast in *this* yeast soup. There are also bacteria! The bacteria in a sourdough starter give bread that taste. That's why it's called *sour*dough! Even though it is a little sour, it is still very yummy!

Yeast is amazing! They create gas bubbles that make bread soft and fluffy. If there were no yeast, how would we get bubbles into bread?

WE NEED A BRAINSTORM

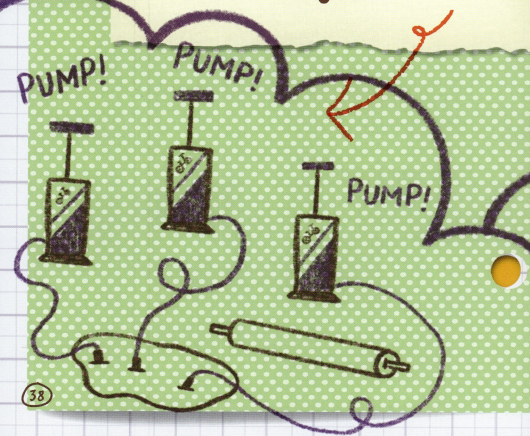

1. We could use itty-bitty bicycle pumps to push air into the dough.

PUMP!

PUMP!

PUMP!

38

2. Teeny, tiny aliens in the dough could chew bubblegum and blow lots of bubbles.

3. We could capture the bubbles in a bath and squish them into the dough.

It is not an ingredient, but bakers also use **heat** to make their treats. Most bakers use an oven to heat and cook their baked goods.

HAVE PEOPLE ALWAYS BAKED BREAD?

Scientists think the first time that humans used ovens to bake bread was in ancient Syria, over 9,000 years ago!

THAT BREAD IS 1,000 TIMES OLDER THAN ME!

SWEET, SWEET SCIENCE

by Ada Twist

Measure the sugar. Measure the milk.

Whip up the batter until it's like silk.

Follow the recipe steps one by one.

Bake in the oven until it is done.

Whether it's cookies or cake that I'm making,

I always use science whenever I'm baking!

Bakers mix *specific* ingredients, in a *specific* order, for a very special result. This mixing of ingredients is called a **reaction**.

Baking soda + lemon = bubbles!

LOTS of baking soda + lemon = LOTS of bubbles!

In science, a reaction is something that makes a change. The mixing of flour and water changes both ingredients into dough. Adding baking powder, baking soda, or yeast to a dough changes it by making it rise.

Bakers who study these reactions are called pastry chefs.

Humans have been baking for thousands of years. But the first modern-day pastry chef is thought to be **MARIE-ANTOINE CARÊME** (1784–1833), who was from France.

One of the first baking schools to open in the United States was run by **ELIZABETH GOODFELLOW** (1767–1851) in Philadelphia. She was well known for her pies and cakes and taught classes at her small school for nearly thirty years.

MALINDA RUSSELL

(1812–unknown) is thought to be the first Black American woman to write a cookbook in the United States. She published her book in 1866. Most of the recipes were for fancy baked desserts!

KIMBERLY BROCK BROWN is an

American pastry chef and became the first Black woman to be included in the American Academy of Chefs.

When I'm baking, I feel like I'm doing science. AM I?

Pastry chefs do a lot of research to make and test each new recipe. They often bake the same thing over and over again. Each time is like an experiment! They make small changes until the final product looks, feels, and tastes exactly how they want.

Pastry chefs use different kinds of science for each new creation.

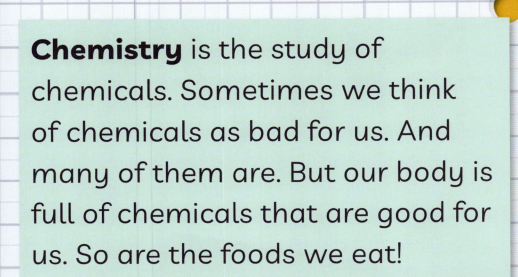

Chemistry is the study of chemicals. Sometimes we think of chemicals as bad for us. And many of them are. But our body is full of chemicals that are good for us. So are the foods we eat!

Sugar, water, baking powder, and baking soda are all examples of chemicals used in baking.

When chemicals mix, it is called a **chemical reaction**. The chemicals come together to make something new. Just like ingredients in a recipe!

It is very important for pastry chefs to understand the chemistry of the foods they are using. This helps them choose just the right ones.

For example, baking powder, baking soda, and yeast are all used to make dough rise. But they *react* differently with the other ingredients in a recipe.

Yeast take a long time to make dough rise. For faster recipes, like those used to make cookies, pastry chefs will use baking powder or baking soda.

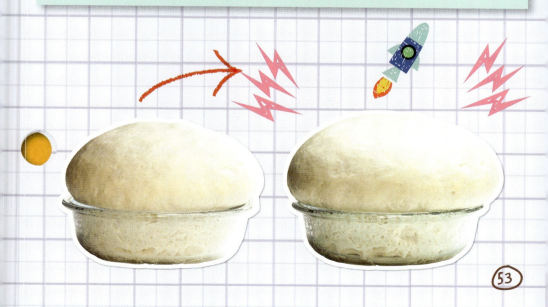

These different chemical reactions make baked goods taste different, too. A pastry chef will choose one depending on the flavor or texture they want their treat to have.

without baking powder!

with baking powder!

Biology is the study of living things, like yeast. Any time a pastry chef uses yeast in a recipe, they are making a **biological reaction**!

Yeast, sugar, and water mix to make something new: air bubbles!

When a pastry chef uses yeast to make dough rise, they have to be very careful. If they let the dough rise for too long, the yeast will eat all the sugar! When this happens, the final result will not have the right flavor.

Physics is the study of how energy and force (a push or pull) affect objects. Pastry chefs use the energy of heat in baking. Heat causes a **physical reaction** to take place. The dough changes! It becomes more solid.

Heat travels from the oven walls to the dough. It moves through the dough by bouncing from air bubble to air bubble. That is how the heat reaches the center. And that's why using baking powder, baking soda, or yeast makes baked goods cook more evenly. Without those bubbles, it is harder for the heat to reach the middle of the dough.

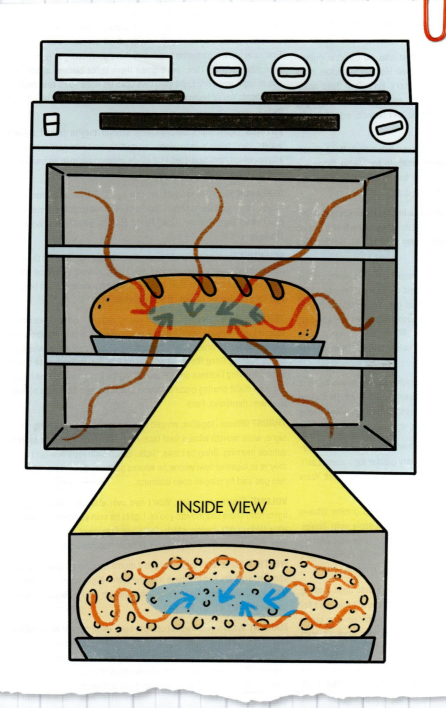

INSIDE VIEW

Math is also very important for pastry chefs! They need to keep track of time and measure their ingredients very carefully. If a recipe is baked too long, it will burn. If it is baked for too little time, it will be raw. Using too little baking powder will make the dough flat. And using too much liquid will make the dough wet and sticky.

Just like scientists, pastry chefs use tools to measure ingredients. They use scales to weigh and special spoons and cups to measure.

Math is important!
2 + 2 = Deliciousness!

Lasheeda Perry is a baker, and she uses science in her job all the time! When she makes baked goods like cookies and cakes, she uses precise measurements of ingredients like baking powder, flour, and butter to make sure her recipes come out just right.

I think I've connected the polka dots! Baking **IS** like doing an experiment. If I use the right amount of the right ingredients in the right way, I'll make the best birthday cake for my dad!

Awesome possum! Who ever thought science could be so yummy?

I have MORE QUESTIONS now than I did before.

Why does each question lead to three questions more?

Is answering that what **science** is for?

MY QUESTIONS!

Why are some cookies crunchy but some are chewy?

Why do burned cookies taste bad?

Do other animals make treats?

Could an astronaut make a cake in space?

Do yeast eat anything besides sugar?

If cake batter includes salt, why doesn't it taste salty?

Why do some things taste salty?

Why do some things taste sweet?

Why do some things taste bitter?

Why do people like different kinds of cakes?

69

SIMPLE SCIENCE EXPERIMENTS

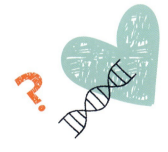

You can ask a grown-up for help!

REACTIONS IN ACTION!

MATERIALS

- 2 clear cups (plastic or glass)

- 1/2 cup of water

- 1/2 cup of vinegar

- 2 tablespoons of baking soda

- Marker

INSTRUCTIONS

1. Label each cup with WATER or VINEGAR.

2. Pour the right liquid into each labeled cup

3. Add 1 tablespoon of baking soda into the cup of water.

4. Observe!

5. Add 1 tablespoon of baking soda into the cup of vinegar.

6. Observe!

What happened? Did baking soda react the same with water as with vinegar? Did both reactions make bubbles? Nope! Baking soda needs to be mixed with an acid (like vinegar) to make bubbles. Share your results on social media using #whyfileswonders!

LET'S TRY ANOTHER EXPERIMENT!

SUGAR COOKIE BAKE-OFF!

MATERIALS

For this experiment, you will use the following list of materials twice to make two separate batches.

- 1/4 cup butter (1/2 cup total)

- 1/3 cup sugar (2/3 cup total)

- 1 egg (2 eggs total)

- 1/2 tablespoon of vanilla extract (1 tablespoon total)

- 1 cup all-purpose flour (2 cups total)

- 1/8 teaspoon salt (1/4 teaspoon total)

- 1/8 teaspoon baking powder (note: you will only use this for one batch)

- Large bowl

- Electric mixer

- Parchment paper

- Rolling pin

- 2 baking sheets

- Oven (use with parental supervision!)

- Cookie cutters or butter knife

INSTRUCTIONS

1. Preheat an oven to 350°F.

2. Wash your hands!

Batch One

1. Soften the butter if needed. Then combine with the sugar in a large bowl using an electric mixer until it becomes creamy.

2. Add the egg and vanilla extract. Mix.

3. Add your dry ingredients: flour, baking powder, and salt.

4. Mix using the electric mixer. When the dough is crumbly, use your hands to mold it into a ball.

5. Place the ball in between two sheets of parchment paper. Use a rolling pin to roll it out to about 1/4 inch thick.

6. Use cookie cutters to cut the dough into shapes. If you don't have cookie cutters, you can use a butterknife to cut the dough into small squares.

Batch Two

Repeat steps 3–9 except **do not** add baking powder to this batch.

Bake

Bake both batches in the oven for 10 minutes. Remove from oven and observe!

What do your cookies look like? Does batch one look different than batch two? Did adding baking powder change your result? Share your results on social media using #whyfileswonders!

Andrea Beaty is

the bestselling author of the Questioneers series and many other books. She has a degree in biology and computer science. Andrea lives outside Chicago where she writes books for kids and plants flowers for birds, bees, and bugs. Learn more about her books at AndreaBeaty.com.

Sirk Productions

Theanne Griffith, PhD,

is a brain scientist by day and a storyteller by night. She is the lead investigator of a neuroscience laboratory at the University of California–Davis and author of the science adventure series *The Magnificent Makers*. She lives in Northern California with her family. Learn more about her STEM-themed books at TheanneGriffith.com.

Chris Lo Bue Photography

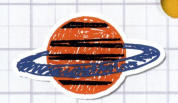

CHECK OUT THESE OTHER BOOKS STARRING
ADA TWIST, SCIENTIST

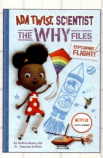

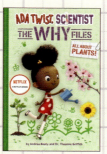

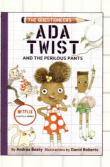

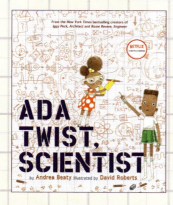

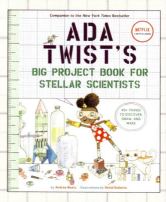

There's more to discover at **Questioneers.com.**